PICCOLO the Pampered Pooch™

Book 1: "Hello World!"

As Piccolo told his story to Head-of-the-Litter,
Author Avery Chenoweth, Sr.

Restoring the innocence of childhood in uplifting, didactic, and heart-warming children's stories as told by the real-life puppies themselves.

A SERIES OF CHILDREN'S STORIES FOR ALL AGES

To include 12 books about Piccolo;
12 about Piccolo's companion, Kool Kuddly Kirk,
and, lastly, 12 about Kirk and Bianca la Bella Bambina

All heartwarming real-life sotries as told by the dogs themselves

Publisher: PPP&K B Inc.;
President & CEO and author:
H. Avery Chenoweth, Sr.

ISBN: 978-0-9846883-5-7
Copyright: 2013

PPP&K/B Inc.,
owns the trademark and all copyrights for the name
and the series of its 36 or more books, and all other
print and eBook properties, as well as designated
art and photography by the author.

Other selected EBook intellectual properties
owned by PPP&K B Inc. include:

"A Guidebook for "Z" Generation Grads"
2014

www.booksbychenoweth.com

BOOK 1
"Hello World..."

As translated by the author,
H. Avery Chenoweth, Sr.,
who explains to pet-loving readers:

This first book — and many yet to come — are what my miniature Italian Greyhound, Piccolo, told me as he reflected on his fascinating, fun-filled, adventurous — but sometimes risky — life.

But, first . . .

You may wonder how my little dog, Piccolo, could dictate a book like this — much less in English.

How can that be? Piccolo did not speak English, he only barked.

Oh, he barked alright. But he thought, too.

I'll share a secret with you: I read Piccolo's mind.

Again, *how?*, you say.

Well, you can do it too with your own pet puppy . . . dog . . . cat . . . guinea pig, rabbit — but not your turtle, or frog, or (ugh!) snake! — cause I don't think those critters like to communicate with us humans.

You can't cuddle those — and cuddling is what's necessary.

There is nothing magic about it. Just hug your pet and whisper into its ear . . . keep telling it you love it . . . and listen carefully. They'll lick your nose or your ear to show that they love you, too.

You see, *Love* transcends all things and so that will allow you to sense your pet's thoughts. And the more you do this, the more you begin to understand what they are trying to tell you. You know, of course, that they already understand a lot of your words anyway.

So . . . just try it.

Here is the first story my dear little Piccolo told me when he was quite old . . .

"First," he said, "you gotta ask your Dear Reader friends: 'Would you believe I'm a hundred and twenty-six years old'?"

"No way," they'd say?

Well, 126 dogs years are 18 human years.

So to me, 18 years old is old age.

Now, at my advanced age, I figured I ought to tell all of them about my life while I still can.

Looking back on it, it has been very pleasant and exciting in lots of ways — *pampered* — I overheard someone say . . . Ahem, I recall that was *you* who are writing this who said that. But, I forgive you. You and Mother-of-the-Litter gave me a wonderful, wonderful life. I couldn't have asked for better.

I will tell them a bunch of stories — some funny, some sad, some scary — but always with happy endings.

So, tell them to sit back and make themselves comfortable . . .

It all began in the beginning:

The first thing I remember was darkness. I didn't know *where* I was — or *what* I was. For that matter, I didn't really know what darkness was either. Something smelled funny — but pleasant.

Then I realized there was a bunch of squiggly-squirmy things pressing all around me, and they were uttering tiny squeals . . . just like I was.

I, too, squirmed and tried to get to the big warm thing I felt close by. Then—suddenly—I felt something gently grab and raise me up and put me down beside the big warm thing right next to something that I put my mouth on and tasted the most wonderful thing imaginable. It was warm and went down my throat and filled my little tummy—and I felt good all over.

And then I forgot everything until my tummy told me it wanted the good warm thing again.

(You realize, of course, that I am remembering all this and it was a long time ago.)

After a while something strange happened. The blackness suddenly went away and it was all bright. Everything was fuzzy for a while, then things appeared. The squiggly-squirmy things turned out to all be little balls of fur just like me, making little squeaky noises — just like me. The big warm thing that I was resting against was soft and cuddly, too, and it made a soothing, slow thump-thump sound which I felt each time it beat. I snuggled up to it as close as I could.

(How could I have known at the time that my eyes had just opened and I could see everything around me? I did not even know what eyes were!)

All of us squiggly-squirmy things were scrunched up together, all snug and warm. When the big thing cuddled up to us, we all scrambled to find the good, warm liquid that we sucked . . . and sucked . . . and that soothed our tiny tummies.

It slowly began to dawn — on me at least — that the big warm thing was just like us — only bigger. And, it sheltered us and was caring for us. So, we stayed close to it and squeaked and fussed when it went away from time to time.

(I realized later that this was something we squiggly things were closely related to. And, too, that all us little squigglers were just alike — except for the different white spots on us. And we all looked just like this big thing — but much, much smaller. The idea of "mother" came from my instinct and I felt a closer attachment.)

All went well for a time. We all cozied up when we slept and struggled to get that delicious, warm goodie that filled our growing tummies. We were all getting a bit bigger, too — and making a lot of noise. I recall, too, that we had to be lifted out now and then to tinkle and poop in a different place. Ugh! — but we felt better afterwards.

(Keep in mind that I am recalling all this — and filling in the blanks here and there.)

We also began to find tiny bits of things in our bowl that tasted yummy in our tummy. When we were thirsty, we found some cool clear water in another bowl that helped wash our food down but didn't taste as good as the sweet stuff from our mother, but she had stopped letting us have it.

Soon, we were getting too big to remain all together on the blanket in our warm little box that was in a much, much larger box where strange smells tickled our little noses. I loved those.

A lot of big creatures kept coming and going, in and out, and they all made peculiar noises. I guess they were barking to each other — but I could not understand them. They would stoop down and pick us up and turn us over — sometimes stick us with something — or wipe us off with a soft thing.

But we did get to scamper and play with each other on the floor of the big room where all those tempting smells from up on the big box that was hot and where something burning were always coming from. We never got any of what ever that was but we did get our own little bits in our big bowl that we voraciously nibbled on — and fast, too, lest one of the other squiggly-squirmers got it first.

So, as we began to grow, the great big creatures that towered above us would move all around us and reach down to pick us up and hug us.

And — sadly —some of us squiggly-squirmers disappeared. Suddenly, one would be picked up by these big moving things and would just vanish. I missed them right away and was very puzzled at their disappearance. Mother seemed a bit upset, too.

One day, I looked around and I was the only squiggly-squirmy left.

I was a tad bit smaller than the rest and they used to always push me away, especially at feeding time. Later, I heard myself called a "runt." I guessed what that meant, but it didn't bother me. I knew who I was now. I figured the best was kept for last.

Then it happened! When Mother and I were quietly nestled together, one of the big moving creatures picked me up, cuddled me and put me in a box with a soft blanket in it. The box lifted up and was taken out in the cool out doors and put into a strange machine that had a smell I had never experienced before — and a roaring sound like no other I'd ever heard before either! I didn't know what was happening. Suddenly I realized that I missed my mother — I felt she must have missed me, too, because I had been her only squiggle-squirmy left.

The box bounced gently for a long while and then stopped. It — with me in it — was lifted again and taken into what I was to learn later was a house. A big, warmer box with all sorts of different smells

— all wonderful and inviting.
I still longed for mother and whimpered a bit.
I heard a lot of strange new sounds — somewhat like those I had heard with all the squigglies — but these were louder and (*if I could have defined them then*) 'happier'. Joyous (*though I did not know what that meant, either*). And they were lighter and song-like and were coming from big creatures that were only half the size of the big tall creatures I was familiar with. I soon forgot all about mother and the other squiggly-squirmies.

Just then, the big thing's two paws (*I learned later that they called them hands*) came into the box and gently grabbed me and took me out and held me up high — right up close to its snout and I looked right into big thing's eyes that were bigger than our squigglies' or even my mother's. And its mouth spread wide and a big squeal came out of it — much louder than I or any of us squigglies could have made. It bared no sharp teeth, so I was not afraid.

Next thing I knew, I was cradled (*I didn't know that term either back then*) in its arms and nestled close to the part of it where it thump-thumped just like Mother's did. It was very comforting and I felt safe and cozy, just like I did when I used to lay close to my Mother in our own box.

I felt other paws *(hands)* petting me and other soothing sounds all around me. I liked very much what was happening and I dozed off right in this creature's arms.

A new sound startled me and I woke up. It was a distinct bark from one of the big creatures. It sounded like "Pick-a-low." I wondered what that meant and I kept hearing them bark it over and over. Whenever one of the big things looked at me, it barked gently, "Pick-a-low"!

It did not take me long to realize that they were calling me that. So, I finally realized that the bark "Piccolo" (*their spelling*) was for me. (*Much, much, later, when I had learned the essence of their barkings — like "treat," "cookie", "food", "pottie," "walkie," "go for a ride" and other key phrases — I overheard them saying that "Piccolo" was an Italian bark for "little." Of course I was little, never more than ten pounds, and — as I overheard them often bark when I was introduced to other big creatures — that I was an "Italian Greyhound." Whatever that is.*)

Piccolo adjusts to a new life

As I got used to this new life, I began to be aware of my surroundings as I was learning to walk, jump and get around while the big creatures watched me and made nice barks that sounded like "Hah, hah!"

They were strange creatures, though. They walked only on their hind legs — not on all four like I did. Their two front legs were high up and they used them for all sorts of things that I could not do — like picking me up.

And they were all different. Each had a different skin that they put on each day. Thank goodness I had only one to fool with: my grey and white one that I always wore. That suited me fine.

I quickly got used to the big creatures and grew close to them. I wanted to be with them all the time. I figured that with my mother — the head of the litter — gone, they must be my new heads of the litter. So, I began in my mind to refer to the bigger and stronger one as "Head-of-the-litter" and softer, cuddlier one as "Mother-of-the-litter." HOL and MOL for short, for I was getting more clever the older I grew. Many times, though, when they sat and watched the strange, noisy box with all the flashing lights — and all the awful barks that went with it — I would hear my own bark — or at least a bark in my own language. I'd perk up my ears, look around the room but never could find the barker like me.

Piccolo grows and grows

(He eats a lot)

I was getting somewhat bigger all the time, too, but I was still awfully skinny. My legs (*that's the bark I heard them call them*) got to be very long, so I was tall. And — Boy! — did I like to run! I would bolt all over the place — around all those strange, big things in the way (*I heard them bark "chairs," "tables," and a "sofa"*). I could jump real high, too.

I especially liked to jump up, though, to settle onto one of their laps now and then for a little snuggle and snooze.

Why do I want to chew all the time?

The hard sharp things in my mouth felt funny and began to hurt. And — I don't know why — but I wanted to chew on everything. First, I tried the edge of the big soft thing on the floor but it tasted awful. The sides of the chairs were pretty good — so were the pillows. But best of all were the chewy things Head- and Mother-of-the-Litter put on their feet. Once, I peeked into a tiny dark room and found all sorts of these things.

One tasted particularly good and I chewed the back off of it. H&MOL were not happy about this. Not at all.

Quickly, they gave me a little white stick to chew on. It was a little like the things they put on their feet but tasted different and were much better to chew — and they last longer and thatseemed to please H&MOL, and me, too.

Also, little things they called "toys" appeared now and then. They were round, some made of soft stuff, some squeaked when I bit down, and all were different. I rollicked all over the house tossing, playing, and chewing on them.

"Walkies"

Every day HOL and MOL would take me for walks outdoors with a collar around my neck with a strap they could hold on to so I would not run away. I would have but not to ever leave them — it's just that I am very curious and would love to dart over and smell something or see something far off and run to investigate. I guess they didn't want me to do that. Anyway, I enjoyed seeing new things and sniffing where other critters like me had been.

At some particular wide space HOL would unhook the strap and let me run free. Oh JOY! *Oh JOY! — did I love that!*

I'd tear off lickety-split as fast as I could — running in a great big circle and come back and whizz past HOL and MOL, watching their broad smiles as I did so. I loved it and I was very obedient and came back when they called me — 'cause I knew that meant a treat for me!

There were so many new smells and something I could not see but could feel all around me . . . sometimes cool, sometimes warm and I could feel it go into my nose and mouth . . . I didn't know what it was but it was very pleasant and refreshing.

One time I happened to look up and saw a big bright light — so bright I had to turn my eyes away! But it did make me feel warm and I liked that.

There were many small things covered with funny little green things all over (*I used that color's name so you could understand, but to me they all looked gray*). And I walked on tiny soft stuff that covered the floor (*ground*) and smelled nice and fresh. I loved to roll over and over in it.

For a time I was fascinated by big — and I mean *really* BIG — and TALL — things that were covered all over with bigger little green things — sometimes with great long things that waved at me and sometimes got in the way of the warm bright thing way, way up high above the tall things.

Another time when we were walking water began to drop on us — and we had to run back to the house. I never could figure that out. One time — much later — I got caught in this water from up above me and I got soaking wet. And, cold, too! I quickly ran back into the house from the back yard and snuggled in my warm bed until I was dry.

I even got my own little bed-house in the big room — a soft-lined box with a roof and I could fit my (*then*) five pounds in it very well to take a nap — which I loved to do when I got tired of playing, and HOL and MOL were watcing the awful noise box or holding square things in their laps and staring at them for hours and hours . . . sometimes with their eyes closed.

But the best part was at dark time — "night" as they barked it. Even though I slept through most of the day —

— but wait! That's a whole new story. I'll tell you all about it next time.

So, the upshot of all this is that this is the way my life started out. And, it turned out to be a very pleasant and exciting one as you will see. I had all sorts of adventures, long trips, scary things, lots of friends sort of like me, and later even a brother, who was a barker like me but who did not resemble me at all. I'll have to tell you all about those later.

One thing, though: HOL and MOL kept barking about my becoming a "pampered pooch." I can't for the life of me figure out what they meant.

Your new friend,

Piccolo

Piccolo the Pampered Pooch™

Book 2: "Learning About Things"

As told to author Avery Chenoweth, Sr. by Piccolo himself

Restoring the innocence of childhood in up-lifting, didactic, and heart-warming real-life stories as told by the puppies themselves.

A SERIES OF CHILDREN'S STORIES FOR ALL AGES

Book 2: Learning About Things

To include 12 books about Piccolo;
12 about Piccolo's companion, Kool Kuddly Kirk,
and, lastly, 12 about Kirk and Bianca la Bella Bambina
All heartwarming real-life sotries as told by the dogs themselves

Publisher: PPP&K B Inc.;
President & CEO and author:
H. Avery Chenoweth, Sr.

ISBN: 978-0-9846883-6-4
Copyright: 2014

PPP&K/B Inc., owns the trademark and all copyrights for the name
and the series of its 36 or more books, and all other
print and eBook properties, as well as designated
art and photography by the author.
Other selected EBook intellectual properties
owned by PPP&K B Inc. include:
"A Guidebook for "Z" Generation Grads"

www.booksbychenoweth.com

Piccolo the Pampered Pooch™   Book 2: Learning About Things

First,
a reminder from Piccolo:

If you remember from Book #1, I told you how old I was (126 in dog years, only 18 in yours), and that I had been telling my life story to my Head-of-the-Litter (HOL) so he could write it down for you. So, here is the second story of my adventurous life that I recalled for him. There will be many more to come . . . so, as they say . . .

"Stay tuned!"

Growing up

My coming into this world that I told you about in my first story was — as I said — the beginning. Little did I know what wonderful things and adventures were in store for me.

Right off the bat I got familiar with my surroundings, with the big space HOL and MOL — I think I'll change and shorten these abbreviations. They are now really "Head-of-the-Pack" and "Mother-of-the-Pack" since that's what the instinct of our species is. You call it "family." So, how about HOP and MOP? That's kinda funny but easier, isn't it? When referring to both of them, I'll call them H&MOP. You like that? . . .

. . . Oh, I almost forgot! At the end of my first book I promised to tell you about bedtime in my new *kennel* — I've got to change that, too, and learn to call it *home*.

So, hang on . . .

My bed-time story

Remember? I promised I would tell you how and where I went to go to sleep every night.

Well, it all started on the first night of the day I was brought as a two-month old puppy to my new home. My new HOP and MOP were trying to be so nice and loving toward me and welcoming me warmly into what would be my home for the rest of my life, although I was too young to grasp it at the time. In addition to my own food and water bowls, that first night they put a large pillow down on the floor next to their bed for me to sleep on.

The pillow — just like the one each of them had up on the big bed — was soft and comfy. After taking me to potty, they gently hugged and kissed me good night before putting me down on it and climbing up onto their bed and falling asleep.

First it was alright . . . then I began to feel lonely. I missed my mommy . . . and I missed being next to her and feeling her thump-thump. So I began to whimper . . . then to cry — and finally to howl at the top of my tiny bark (voice)! I would do this over and over again all night long. I heard H&MOP stir and turn and bark in low tones above me from time to time — but nothing happened. I never moved from my pillow but did not sleep at all. I guessed H&MOP didn't get any sleep either.

They did not appear happy the next morning.

The second night

The next night when bed time came and they turned off the awful noisy box and the lights in the rooms, something different happened: H&MOP picked me up, took me to my potty and — THEN INTO THE BIG BED WITH THEM!

Even before they could settle themselves, I scrunched myself down under the covers down to where their lower paws (feet) would be . . . and curled up to go to sleep — without doing my six turn-arounds that for some reason I always wanted to do.

H&MOP raised the covers to check on me and barked something quietly. Then we all fell fast asleep and woke up the next morning fresh and happy.

The upshot

So what happened after that? What happened was that from that second night I slept every night in the big high bed with both H&MOP for all the rest of the eighteen years of my life. I slept mostly under HOP's left armpit, or sprawled between them, or nestled up against

MOP's body . . . or sometimes down at their feet. They flapped the covers now and then to give me some fresh air . . . only that just caused me to stir a bit. At times HOP made awful noises from his snout as he slept but I learned to sleep right through them.

Now, every evening, when H&MOP get up to go to bed, I jump off one of their laps and beeline it to the bed — **OOPS**! — no, first I do my potty by myself, *then* hop up in the big bed and snuggle under the covers waiting for them. It's nice and warm and snuggly there under the covers with them — just like when I was with my mother.

    I heard them say one day that my breed, the Italian Greyhound, is a natural "bed-warmer" and loves to burrow. That must be why I like this so much.

My big playground

The big box that was my new home had many other smaller boxes that H&MOP called "rooms."

    I loved to scamper about from one to another. One time I went too fast around a corner and skidded into a chair! I hurt myself and cried out. HOP came running to me and gingerly picked me up and held me close to him gently rubbing my sore spot — which he called a "bobo" — softly barking into my ear that everything would be alright.

Both H&MOP held me like that a lot . . . and I loved it. It made me feel good and safe and know that they loved me.

A mysterious trip

One day, H&MOP were particularly attentive to me. After I ate and pottied, they put my leash on me. I was happy because I thought we were going for our walk.

Instead, we all got into the car and MOP held me in her lap, on top of the straps she had around her waist and shoulders.

They were unusually quiet and I wondered what was going on.

Soon we arrived at a small building and we all got out and went inside. It smelled kinda funny — like I never smelled before. And, sitting on the floor next to chairs or in their pack leaders' laps (I guessed) were other small and large critters — none like me — some tinier (if you can believe that!), some really, really big. They were all quiet, though. I supposed well-behaved . . . like me.

In a little cage off to the side was something dark and fluffy and it made a soft purring sound, not at all like my barks.

We joined them and I stared at them in wonder. They were a strange lot but seemed friendly.

After a while some big creature came up and softly barked a few words at my H&MOPs, scooped me up (the right way) and took me away . . .

. . . the next thing I knew they laid me down on a warm cloth on a table and stuck something in my neck.

From that moment on I don't remember a thing.

It must have been some time later that I woke up and felt like I had taken a nap. Slowly I came back to my old self, Piccolo . . . but then again, I wasn't quite my old self. Something felt like it was missing but I didn't hurt anywhere. Much later, though, I did feel some tingling sensation right under my rump for a short while . . . but the big change was that I felt calmer. And I was OK with that.

I got stuck with something sharp a couple more times in the back of my neck and on a leg, and somebody put a little jingly thing onto my leash collar.

On the way home I dozed off right in MOP's lap.

As I was observing and learning something new every day, I began to understand H&MOP's barks. They didn't bark like me — I barked loud and sharp. Their's were totally different. And they strung them together and they sounded nice and pleasant . . . and that intrigued me. Once or twice, though, HOP would sort of growl and it would startle me. But soon I began to understand their barks — which I heard them call "words."

Of course, right away I had understood that "Piccolo" was what they called me. And I figured out what "Come here" and "Oh-oh" meant . . . also "treat" and "cookie" and "Let's go for a walk"—

which they called a "walkie" . . . and that other necessary thing they called "potty time."

"Pottie time" didn't take long for me to understand. From the first, they would pick me up and take me to a special box placed on the floor of a funny room where they went to do their potty — and to take off their skins and get under a fountain of water . . . then come out and dry off with a big fluffy thing and put on new skins that were different each time. It took me a long time to figure out that those were not their skins — nothing like mine that I didn't have to change. No, they were coverings over their skins and they were all sorts of colors . . . although I could only detect a few, I discovered.

. . . But I digress. My potty box was filled with big thin things of something they called "papers" — "newspapers." And I would do my "business" — OK — *tinkle and poop*! Every big creature and all others I came across in life have to do *that*, so it is nothing to be embarrassed about. You just do your 'business' in private — not in front of people.

Right after I finished by business it would disappear and fresh papers would be put down for the next time. H&MOP called it my "Pitty Pot." I also discovered that I could tinkle and poop out doors in the yard and nobody would mind so long as it was off somewhere away from the house and the sidewalks.

Meeting other creatures

I had already observed that H&MOP and other big creatures like them walked only on their two hind legs. My next discovery was that some of their very little ones did, indeed, walk on all four legs — but not quite like I do.

One day some big creatures came to visit and carried with them in their two top legs ("arms" I heard them call them later) a small creature somewhat like them. The little thing made funny noises and blew tiny bubbles out of its snout and when they put it down on the floor for me to sniff, it crawled away on all fours!

But not nearly as fast as I could. I darted around it in circles and sniffing it, happy that at last I had found a playmate!

But it was not to be. Suddenly my new playmate made an ugly noise and began to stink real bad . . . then barked real loud before it was scooped up and whisked away to the pitty-pot.

Oh, well . . .

To my surprise, when the big creature came back with my new friend, it was not stinky anymore. Now it smelled sweet and nice and made happy sounds.

    Another surprise: the big creature held the little one close to her and the tiny one stopped wiggling and made cooing and sucking sounds . . . and it made me think of the sweet thing from my own mother that used to fill my tiny tummy. It seems all mother creatures do this wonderful thing with their babies.

More things to learn

I was growing every day; soon I would reach my full size: ten pounds, as I overheard H&MOP say. My long legs were really long and my neck was long, too. My body looked funny because my chest was big and my hind quarters were very thin, and I had a long skinny tail that wanted to wig-wag back and forth all the time — when I was happy — which was always.

I could run fast and jump high, high enough to get on the tables sometimes — before being scooted off. On our walks every day I would meet other little — and some big — critters like me — but not exactly. I could understand their barks and most were friendly except for one or two meany ones. Some were all hairy and furry and some were tiny and skinny. One named Taco el Chihuahua was even smaller than me. There was a different critter, too, that was my size but was soft and slinky and was not friendly at all. It didn't bark either but made a soft sort of "Meow" sound and hissed at me. I left that one alone.

My favorite new friend was my size but his legs had not grown — they were short and his belly was close to the ground. We liked to run and chase each other — but I ran circles around him while the big creatures stood by and laughed. I heard them call my new friend a "sausage dog." I didn't know what that meant, but we always had fun anyway.

Piccolo the Pampered Pooch meets his cousins

One day H&MOP put my collar and leash on me and we all got into the car (by then I knew to call it that and I loved to ride and look out at the whizzing things and the big boxes, and the big blue area up above). I heard them say we were going to a Dog Show.

A "Dog Show?" What was that? I had heard them often say they were going to watch a "show" on the big flashing-squawking box they sat in front of for long times, so I figured this must be something like that . . . dogs (which I had realized by then was what I was) making a lot of noise and flashing lights.

HOP drove the car and I sat in MOPs lap (no seat belt laws back then). Out of the window I suddenly saw a big, big box — much bigger than the box we all lived in — and we stopped near it.

As we all got out and walked — me on my leash, of course — I noticed many other critters — "dogs" I called them now — some looking kinda like me only not. At least they all walked properly on all four legs like me and had tails but were of all shapes and sizes like I had never seen before.

We went inside a big, big, noisy room that almost terrified me. Noticing this, MOP picked me up and held me in her arms (by then I knew they called them "arms") and we walked around to see all the dogs and their H&MOPs. My eyes were about to pop out just seeing all these strange things and hearing all these new sounds.

At one point we stopped and MOP put me down. I was startled. There in front of me were two dogs that looked just like me. I knew how I looked because our front door at our house had a strange thing on it so that when I looked out I saw another dog just like me.

Every time I would go up to the door, so would the dog that looked just like me — and he would do everything I would do — except bark. I would look at him and he would bark at the same time I would but I could not hear him. Very strange. I would move and he would move just like me. I would turn and walk away and he would do the same thing. I put my nose right up to his and he did the same thing. I wanted to play with him but he was stubborn and just mocked me in everything I did. After a number of these encounters, it finally dawned on me that that was ME! — especially when MOP came up behind and in front of me and I saw both of us! I figured there could not be two MOPs so I guessed I was seeing myself. And, so I got to see what I looked like.

And I was not disappointed, if I do say so, myself. That door became on of my favorite tricks; I would play seeing myself doing all sorts of jumps and spins.

So . . . back to these two dogs that looked like me. One was twice a big as me, the other was even bigger than that! But we all looked alike. What gives?

MOP looked down at me and said, "Piccolo, meet your cousins."

I caught what she meant and was startled.

"This small one here — "Wilma the Whippet" is two times bigger than you. And the big one is "Greg the Greyhound" — a racing greyhound — four times bigger. You are all Greyhounds. You, Piccolo, are an Italian Greyhound, too, and the smallest. So, you are all cousins; you look alike, you run alike, your temperaments are alike — it's just your sizes are different."

I found that very interesting, to say the least. I told my new cousins in my own bark how delighted I was to meet them and asked if we could all three go out and run and play.

"Not allowed to," they quickly countered. They explained they were professionals, who had to work at these shows to earn prizes to please their H&MOPs. They spent a lot of their time in cages going from one show to another all over the place. Plenty of time to relax but not much to visit and play.

I relished in the thought that there was something new to discover every day. And, I soaked up knowledge (if I had known that word then) about everything I saw or sniffed around me. I always went to bed each night in anticipation of what the next day would bring. What a wonderful world this was turning out to be!

Next time I'll tell you about loving to take rides in the car and about a little accident I had when I drank something I should not have.

Your friend,
Piccolo

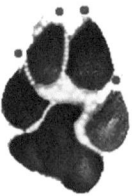

PICCOLO THE PAMPERED POOCH™

A SERIES OF CHILDREN'S STORIES FOR ALL AGES

To include 12 books about Piccolo;
12 books about Piccolo's companion, Kool Kuddly Kirk,
and, lastly, 12 about Kirk and Bianca la Bella Bambina.

All heartwarming real-life stories as told by the pups themselves

Publisher: PPP&K B Inc.
President & CEO and Author:
H. Avery Chenoweth, Sr.

ISBN: 978-0-9846883-8-8
Copyright 2014

PPP&K B Inc.,
owns the trademark and all copyrights for the name and
series of its 36 or more books, and all other print
and eBook properties, as well as designated
art and photography by the author.

Other selected EBook intellectual properties
owned by PPP&K B Inc. include:

"A Guidebook for **Z Generation** Grads"
2014

www.booksbychenoweth.com

"But—
Before we
start…"

Well, my dear readers, if HOP (Head-of-the-Pack) — WAIT! You know? I think I'll even drop that **Head-** and **Mother-of-the-Pack** business. They are really my Mom and Dad now, since I have heard them call themselves that. Yes, my **new Mom** and my **new Dad**!

So, if "Dad" is translating and writing down all of what I have been recalling to him in the previous two stories, you should have a pretty good idea as to how my wonderful — and, I mean it was full of wonder — life started out.

Yes, in that first year — as I was growing to about seven years old in dog years — I had a joyous time. I frolicked about, chased my toys, chewed on my chewies . . . by the way, one of my favorites was a flat, round thing that squeaked when I bit it in the right place. It was tan on top and bottom and yellow and red in the middle. I heard Dad & Mom call it my hamburger. I saw them eat things that looked like my toy but I could not eat *my* hamburger — my teeth would not cut into it — they just bounced back. All I could do was toss it in the air over and over and run and bite to hear it squeak.

Being picked up

There was one thing I dreaded though — being picked up the wrong way.

Whenever other creatures came to visit — especially the little ones — or even on our walks — they tried to pick me up. They would face me and put their paws (hands) under my front legs and lift me just like they did their own babies — and that hurt! Then, they would cradle me in their arms upside down and I did not know where I was or how far up I was. It scared me and was very uncomfortable . . . and, of course, as tiny and skinny as I am, I am not as strong physically — but surely strong *willed*! — as other dogs, so my legs or tail could easily break. I have to be cautious all the time.

Mom & Dad knew how to pick me up the right way. They bent over behind me and put a hand under my chest and the other under my hind legs

and then gently lifted me, holding me rightside up in their folded and secure arms so I could see what was going on. When they put me down, they did so gently and it did not hurt my paws (feet).

I wish everybody knew how to pick us up the right way. Maybe after reading this, they will do so with their own pets.

A wonderful surprise

I had a big surprise one summer day. Mom and Dad leashed me up and we all got into the car. It was a little different than usual, though. Mom and Dad — I'll call them "M & D" from now on—brought some strange stuff with us. First, I noticed was my food bowl. Hmmm . . . how's that? Then, there were some little clear bottles of something I couldn't tell . . . until later when to my delight I discovered they were filled with cool water.

Then there was a funny little box, which I found out later contained my food and theirs, too. But the thing was — they brought my treats along, too, so I knew it was going to be a very pleasant day.

But when we got to where we were going — WOW! I did not expect to see something blue stretching out as far as I could see. No trees, no grass, no land, no houses, no cars — only blank, flat, blue that never ended. What in the world?

And we stepped down onto a lot of white dirt that went right down to the moving edge of the big blue thing. And behind the moving back and forth edge were some white things that came up from nowhere and crashed back down with loud noises . . . and it did this over and over and over.

This all frightened me at first but Mom held the leash real tight so I knew nothing could happed to me.

I was puzzled by the soft white ground. Where it was real soft it was kind'a hard to walk in. Then it got harder and wetter the closer we walked to the moving edge of the big noisy things that would come and go and roll towards us and then go back . . . and do this over and over . . . and over again.

A bunch of white things whizzed all around us and rose up off the ground, and flapping their big wide arms, they went up and down and all around above us, making squawking noises with their long pointed snouts. I wondered how they could ever do such a thing — I tried but I could not do anything but jump up a good way before fallng back on my paws. Huh.

Crazier than that, both the big and the small things that flittered all over our heads would go a little higher up then suddenly drop right straight down into the blue stuff . . . would disappear . . . then suddenly pop up with something in their pointed snouts and flap away off out of sight.

Amazing!

Another surprise! We got closer to the strange moving edge and I thought it looked like water, but not like the water in my water bowl at home . . . this had tiny bubbles in it. Mom and Dad stepped right into the moving edge with me in tow — it WAS water!

It covered my paws and swirled around me and I loved it! I even chased some of the bubbles.

We all splashed our paws and feet in it and began to dance and cavort (*Dear reader, you know I could not have known those words back then before I was a year old — seven years to you — but now as I am telling you this in my old age those are the best ones to describe the joyous feelings we had*).

I began to wonder, too, since this did feel like water. I looked around and all I could see was water . . . water . . . water everywhere — but there was so much of it — where did it come from?

Curious critter that I was (and still am), I thought, OK, water . . . and I am thirsty . . . so? I bent down an lapped some —

— YIPES! What a taste! Awful!

My snout puckered up and I couldn't swallow — so I spit it out! And it sort a burned my tongue. It sure wasn't like MY water!

Dad and Mom laughed and wagged a finger at me, which I knew meant "No. no!" I got the idea. Never again. Funny, too, that taste made me thirtier than ever. I couldn't wait to get back to the car and drink some real water in my own bowl.

I thought to myself: all that wonderful water and you can't drink it. All I saw were creatures floating, and moving and romping and splashing in it, and a lot of small creatures squealing and digging in the strange white dirt. So I guess all that water was just for fun. Yep, I'll buy that . . . I even enjoyed splahing around in it myself.

The only bad thing was it began to make my skin itch. Luckily, when we went back to the car, before getting in, we all stood together under some more sprinkly water like the one in our potty room at home and with much better water, and rinsed the yukkie big blue water off ourselves.

I understood Dad to say we had to rinse the salt water off of us.

SALT? What was that? I had never tasted salt before . . . and I did kinda like it — but in that big blue water thing — **Ugh!**

Piccolo the Pampered Pooch — Book 3: "Oh, Oh—I was naughty!"

Then we dried off and drove home. I felt so relaxed and happy that I fell fast asleep right away in Mom's lap.

Oh, oh!

All that good time — and others went down the drain because one day I did something I should not have: **I was naughty.**

It was late one sunny afternoon, Mom and I — *me in her lap, of course* — were sitting in a big rocking chair on the front porch enjoying the cool breeze and listening to the little things that darted about in the air chirping their catchy tweets as the big round hot thing way up in the sky began to cool off and drop down out of sight.

Every now and then Mom would lower the square thing she had been staring at to take a sip from a funny looking glass on the table next to the chair. I, of course, was puzzled as to what she was drinking.

Suddenly, a *Brrrinnnng! Brrrinnng!* came ringing from inside the house and Mom put the square thing on the table next to the funny glass and rushed through the doorway. I could hear her soft barks that she made into the little black thing she held to her ear and mouth. They went on and on . . . and . . . and on and on . . . so I got bored. And, would you know, curious creature that I am, I decided to find out what it was in the funny glass that she was sipping. She seemed to like it, maybe I would like it, too.

So, I stood up in the chair and put my two front paws on the little table . . . and sniffed the funny thing. It didn't smell all that good but I stuck my tongue into it anyway and lapped up some of it.

It didn't taste very good either and I sort of gagged as it went down into my tummy. I was thirsty, though, so I kept lapping it. I thought it must be OK since Mom had done the same thing — not *lapping*, of course but sipping out of the funny glass.

Well, in a short time I was licking the bottom of the funny glass. All of the watery stuff was gone.

Suddenly I felt dizzy and could hardly sit myself down again. I felt real sleepy, too, and rested my head over the edge of the seat — and don't remember anything at all after that — except that I do recall feeling sick and up-

Piccolo the Pampered Pooch — Book 3: "Oh, Oh—I was naughty!"

chucking right onto the floor. I stayed woozy, too. Everything kept sort of spinning around it seemed. AND — NO! — I DID NOT LIKE IT ONE BIT! AND MY HEAD BEGAN TO HURT SOMETHING AWFUL!

After Mom cleaned up my mess, she wrapped me in a towel and let me sleep in her lap for a long, long time until I felt better. As I recall, it was a very, very long time before I really felt good again.

During all this, I vaguely remember she kept touching me gently from time to time but even that did not wake me up. Later, I overheard her tell Dad when he returned home something about the "Vet" . . . and that she thought I had died. I was so limp and unresponsive.

He laughed and replied that, Yes, I was — *dead* drunk!

One thing that this bad episode taught me was NEVER — EVER to drink anything again that is not in my own water bowl or is not offered to me ONLY by Mom or Dad.

My little body is fragile — and precious — and can only take so much — and some things can hurt you forever. There was something in that bad stuff I drank that did hurt me. From that time throughout the rest of my life my little tummy would not feel right sometimes and I would have to be taken to the dog-doctor (the "Vet") . . . who would sting my neck with something and give me some little things to swallow. These little things tasted bitter and I retched at trying to take them, so Mom would put them in a little chunk of cheese — which I loved — and I swallowed them right down. Sometimes she would put the tiny thing in some peanut butter and that was goo, too.

My little learning experience here applied only to drinking. Next time I will tell you another lesson I learned the hard way about **eating** something I should not have . . . but it *tasted sooooo good!* . . . and made me soooo sick!

So, till next time,

Your friend,

Piccolo

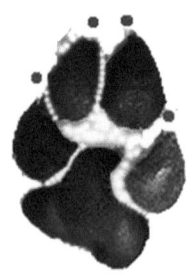

www.ingramcontent.com/pod-product-compliance
Lightning Source LLC
Chambersburg PA
CBHW061357090426
42743CB00002B/41